CAN YOU FIND MY LOVE?™

BUGS

JAN MARQUART

www.CanYouFindMyLove.com

ISBN: 0996854142
ISBN-13: 9780996854146

Cover and Interior by Publish Pros
www.publishpros.com

Books currently available in the "Can You Find My Love?" Series

Seasons: Book1

Things To Do Outside: Book 2

Why We Need Rain: Book3

Things With Wheels: Book 4

Families: Book 5

Bugs: Book 6

Other Books by Jan Marquart

FOR ADULTS

Write to Heal

The Mindful Writer, Still the Mind, Free the Pen

The Basket Weaver, a Novel

Kate's Way, a Novel

Echoes from the Womb, a Book for Daughters

Voices from the Land

The Breath of Dawn, a Journey of Everyday Blessings

How to Write From Your Heart (booklet)

How to Write Your Own Memoir (booklet)

A Manual on How to Deal With a Bully in the Workplace

Cracked Open, a Book of Poems

A Writer's Wisdom

To:

_____

NAME

It is with great respect that I acknowledge the work of Rich Carnahan of Publish Pros for the continued effort in designing, editing and promoting the Can You Find My Love? children's theme-based book series.

To master Aiden Pearce, whose fascination with this series provokes useful comments, suggestions and interest, a huge hug and a warm thank you.

CAN YOU FIND MY LOVE?
is dedicated to all children.

May each child be filled
with love and the fun for learning.

You have received this book
because someone loves you.

Look closely—you will find love hidden
in everyday things that you might
normally take for granted.

This is what it looks like.

♥

When you find the love I have placed
for you, I hope that it warms your
heart and lets you know how
very special you are.

Each BUG has its own beauty.
Look closely.

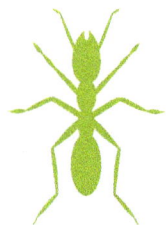

BUGS

STINK BUGS

These bugs give off a stinky smell when they
want to protect their homes.

CAN YOU FIND MY LOVE?

DRAGON FLIES

Dragonflies are expert fliers. They can turn, hover and move backward like a helicopter.

CAN YOU FIND MY LOVE?

CENTIPEDES

Centipedes can usually be found hidden
under rocks and leaves or inside rotting wood.

LADYBUGS

Ladybugs are red beetles that can have up to twenty black spots on their backs.

CAN YOU FIND MY LOVE?

BUMBLE BEES

Bumble bees are large, fuzzy
and can fly longer than other bees.

JUNE BEETLES

June beetles are shiny like metal
and munch on leaves at night.

FLIES

Most flying insects have four wings, but flies buzz around with only two.

BUTTERFLIES

Butterflies come in many colors
and drink a flower's juice with their feet.

CAN YOU FIND MY LOVE?

LIGHTNING BUGS

Lightning bugs, also called fireflies,
talk to each other by blinking their butts.

CAN YOU FIND MY LOVE?

PRAYING MANTIS

The praying mantis is the only insect that can turn its head to look over its shoulder.

CAN YOU FIND MY LOVE?

COCKROACHES

While you usually see them running,
cockroaches do have wings and most can fly.

CAN YOU FIND MY LOVE?

MOSQUITOES

Mosquitoes are attracted to your breath,
and only the girl mosquito bites.

CAN YOU FIND MY LOVE?

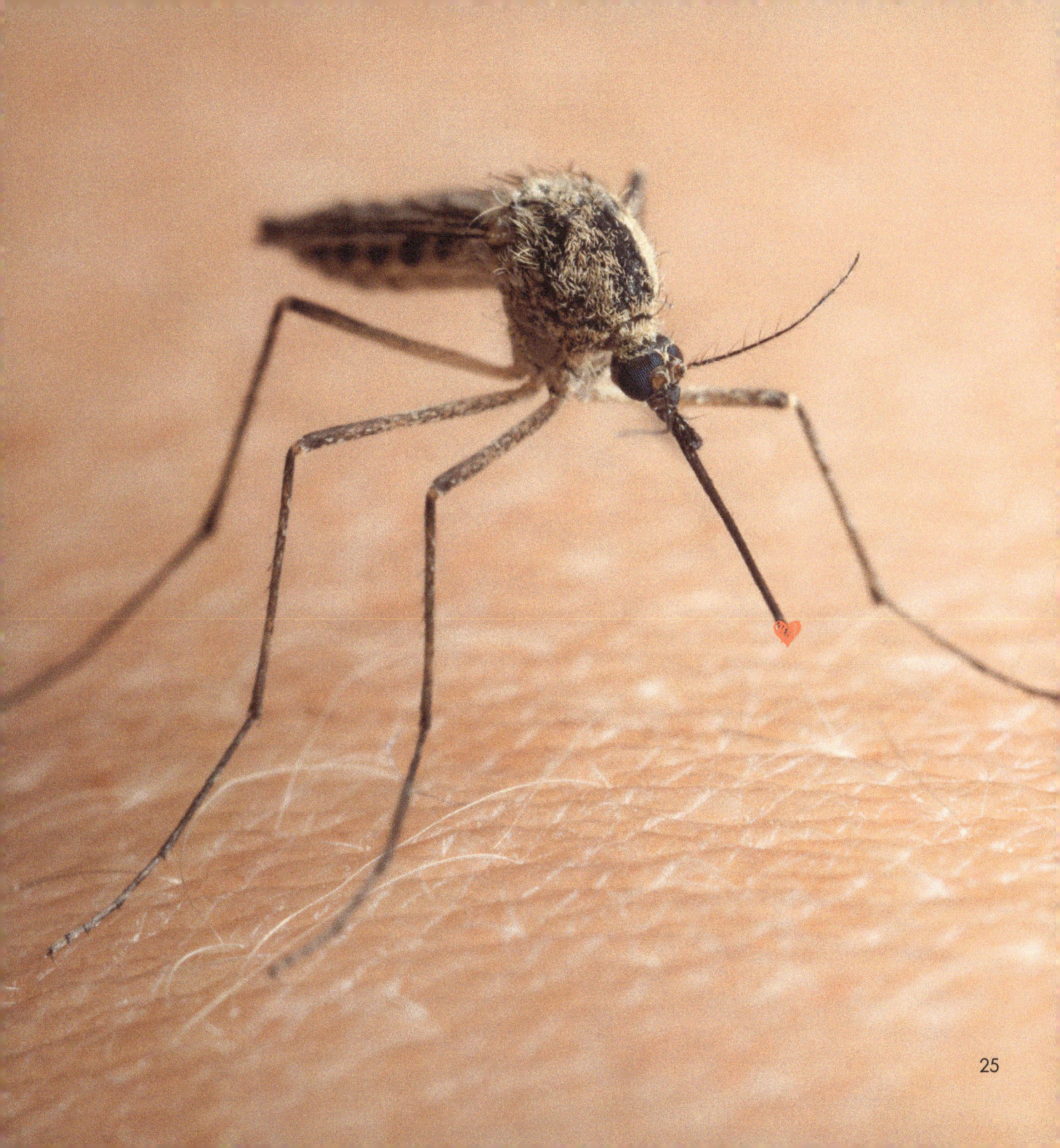

STICK BUGS

Stick bugs can change color to blend in
with their environment.

CAN YOU FIND MY LOVE?

SPIDERS

Spiders make sticky webs
to trap other bugs for their dinner.

MOThS

Moths are related to butterflies
and are attracted to bright light.

BEES

Bees are the only insects that
make food that humans eat—honey!

CAN YOU FIND MY LOVE?

CRICKETS

Male crickets rub their front wings together
to make a chirping sound.

SOW BUGS

Sow bugs, also called pill bugs,
roll into a little ball when they get scared.

CAN YOU FIND MY LOVE?

ANTS

Ants can carry twenty times their own weight.
That's like you carrying a refridgerator.

WASPS

Wasps live almost everywhere
and make paper nests from tree wood.

CAN YOU FIND MY LOVE?

GRASShOPPERS

Grasshoppers can leap twenty times
as far as their body length.

CAN YOU FIND MY LOVE?

Did you look close enough
to find all my love?

Can you **DRAW** a few other **BUGS**?

Can you **DRAW** a few other **BUGS**?

Can you **DRAW** a few other **BUGS**?

From:

paste
photo
here

_____

NAME

About the Author

Jan Marquart is a psychotherapist and author. She has published 11 books for adults and has had articles, stories, poems and essays published in various newspapers, journals and magazines across the United States, Australia and Europe. She teaches writing for those over fifty and has taught a dozen writing workshops for Story Circle Network.

Jan has designed a 6-week writing course titled *Unveil the Wounded Self - Write to Heal* which focuses on healing PTSD and has also designed a 6-week writing course titled *The Provocation of Journal Writing* to encourage everyone to write their personal stories. She is currently on her 99th daily journal.

Jan can be contacted at JanMarquart.com, JanMarquartlcsw.wordpress.com and at her personal email address, jan@canyoufindmylove.com.

Her books can be purchased from all major online book retailers.

www.ingramcontent.com/pod-product-compliance
Lightning Source LLC
Chambersburg PA
CBHW040247100426
42811CB00011B/1186

9780996854146